THE LORD'S PRAYER

Illustrated by

TIM LADWIG

EERDMANS BOOKS FOR YOUNG READERS
GRAND RAPIDS, MICHIGAN / CAMBRIDGE, U.K.

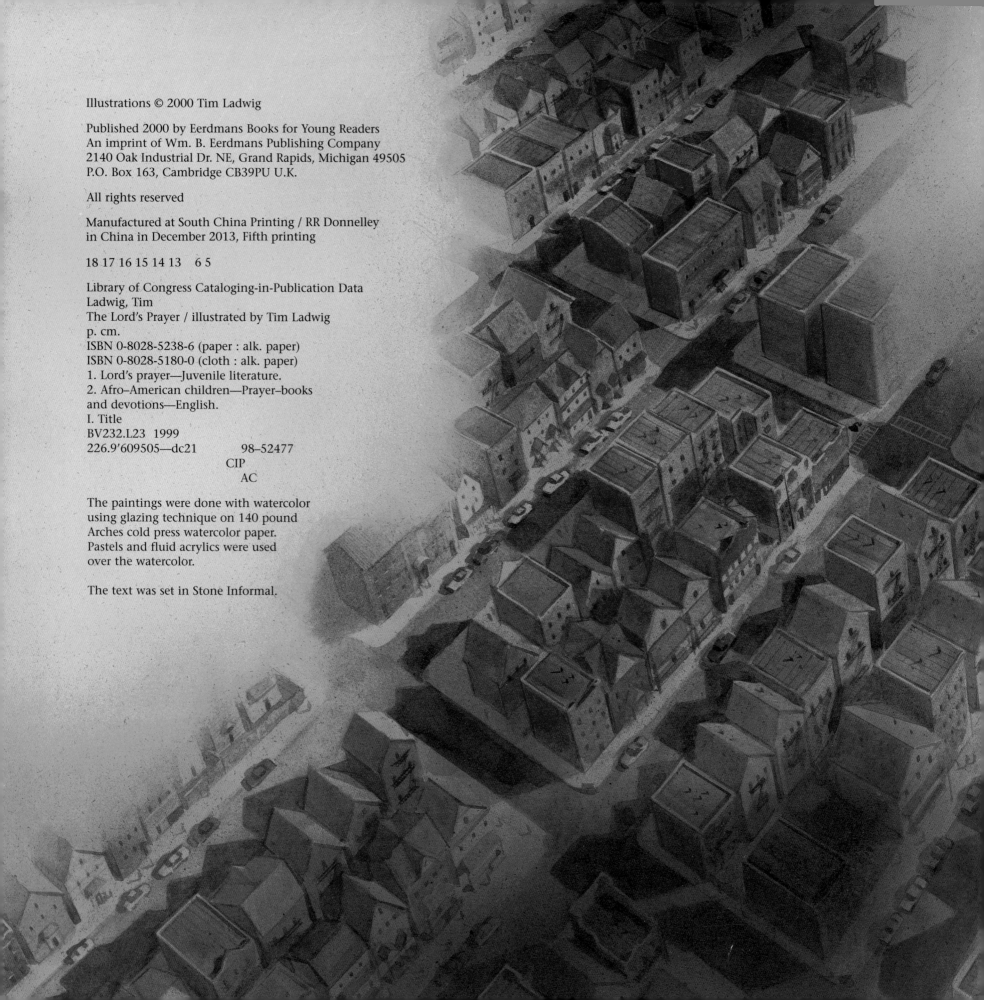

Illustrations © 2000 Tim Ladwig

Published 2000 by Eerdmans Books for Young Readers
An imprint of Wm. B. Eerdmans Publishing Company
2140 Oak Industrial Dr. NE, Grand Rapids, Michigan 49505
P.O. Box 163, Cambridge CB39PU U.K.

Manufactured at South China Printing / RR Donnelley
in China in December 2013, Fifth printing

18 17 16 15 14 13   6 5

Library of Congress Cataloging-in-Publication Data
Ladwig, Tim
The Lord's Prayer / illustrated by Tim Ladwig
p. cm.
ISBN 0-8028-5238-6 (paper : alk. paper)
ISBN 0-8028-5180-0 (cloth : alk. paper)
1. Lord's prayer—Juvenile literature.
2. Afro–American children—Prayer–books
and devotions—English.
I. Title
BV232.L23 1999
226.9'609505—dc21   98–52477
                    CIP
                     AC

The paintings were done with watercolor
using glazing technique on 140 pound
Arches cold press watercolor paper.
Pastels and fluid acrylics were used
over the watercolor.

The text was set in Stone Informal.

To Don Davis
and in memory of his father, Mr. Ted Davis.
They have both taught us who our Father is.

—T. L.

Our Father in heaven,

hallowed be your name.

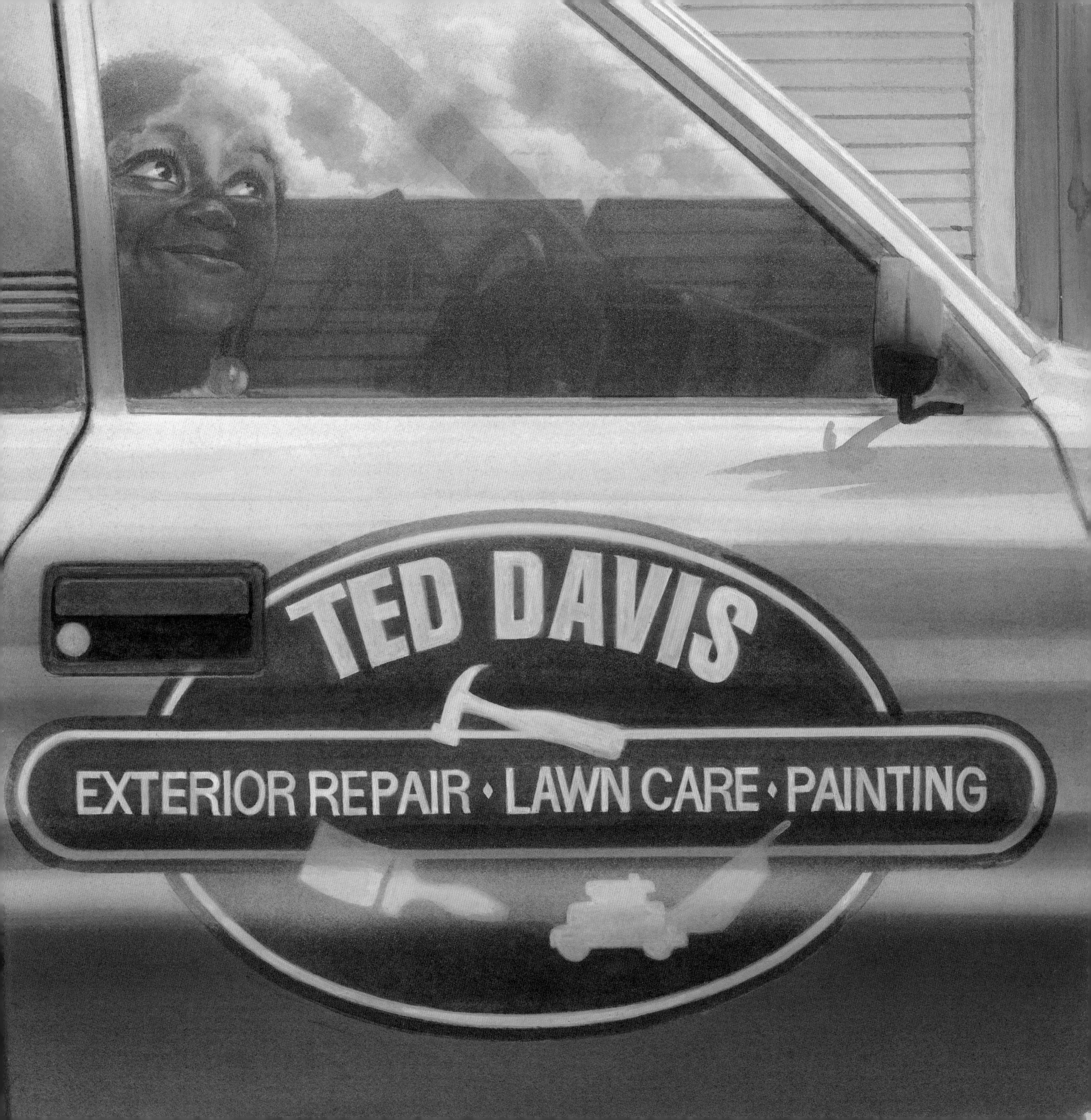
TED DAVIS
EXTERIOR REPAIR • LAWN CARE • PAINTING

Your kingdom come.

Your will be done

on earth as it is in heaven.

Give us this day our daily bread.

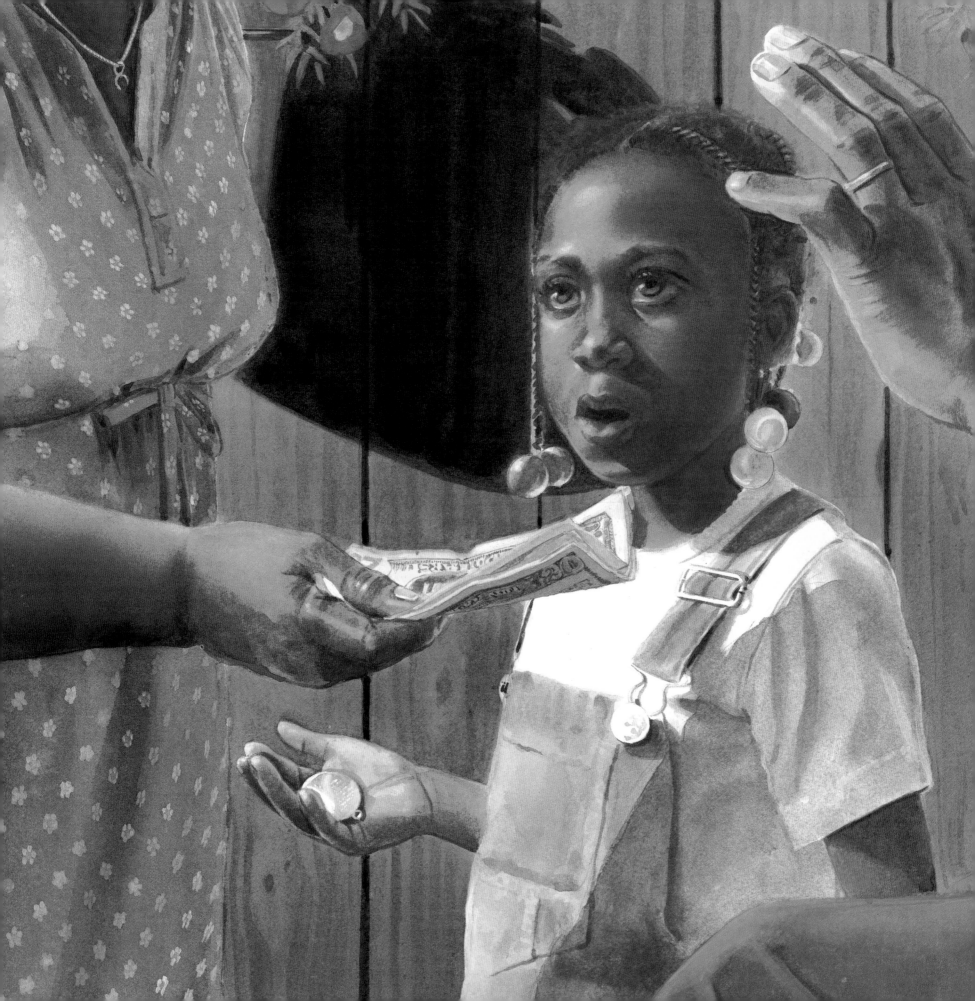

And forgive us our debts
as we forgive our debtors.

And lead us not into temptation,
but deliver us from evil.

For yours
is the kingdom,
and the power,
and the glory

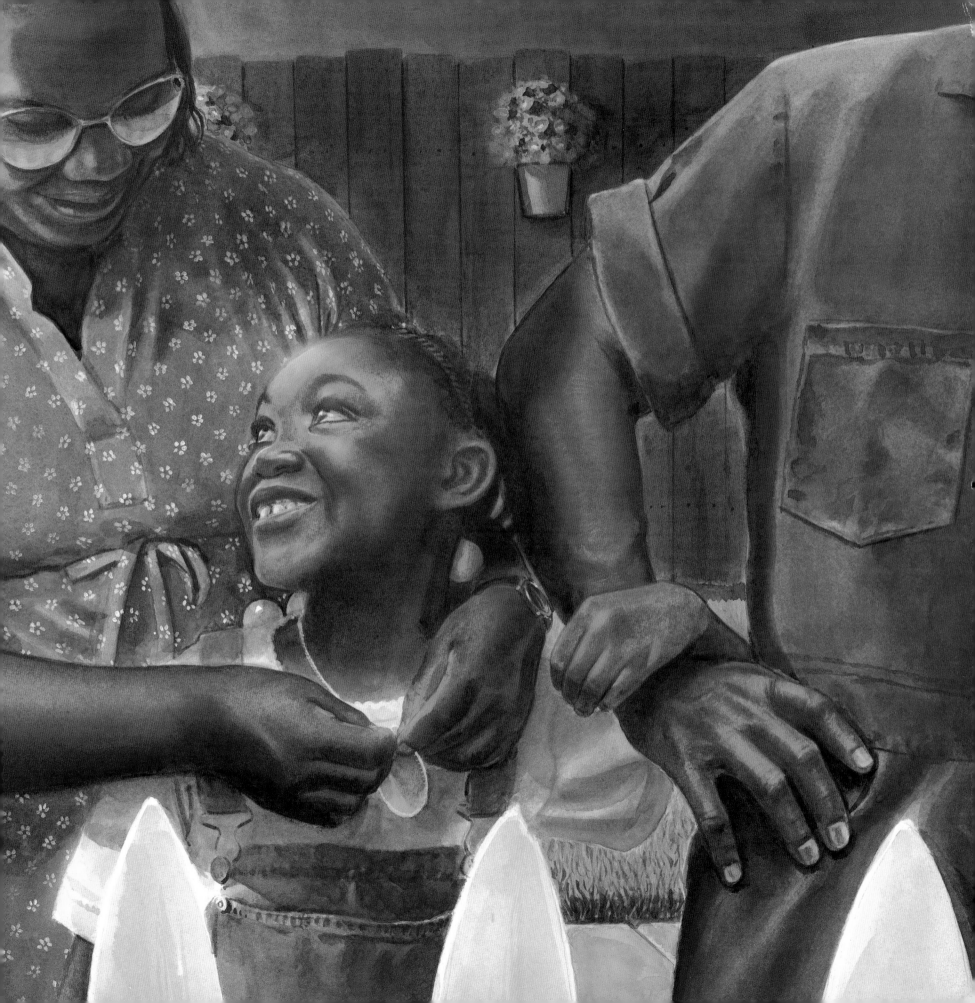

forever.

Amen.